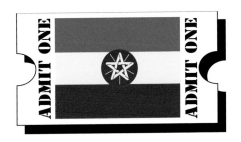

Hills
Surrounding
The Village
Of Konso

FACES
AND
PLACES

ETHIOPIA

BY ELMA SCHEMENAUER

THE CHILD'S WORLD®, INC.

GRAPHIC DESIGN AND PRODUCTION
Robert E. Bonaker / Graphic Design & Consulting Co.

PHOTO RESEARCH
James R. Rothaus / James R. Rothaus & Associates

COVER PHOTO
Portrait of a young Amaha girl
by: CORBIS/ Diego Lezama Orezzoli

Library of Congress Cataloging-in-Publication Data
Schemenauer, Elma.
Ethiopia / by Elma Schemenauer.
p. cm.
Includes index.
Summary: Describes the history, geography, people, and
customs of Ethiopia.
ISBN 1-56766-713-9 (lib. bdg. : alk. paper)

1. Ethiopia — Juvenile literature.
[1. Ethiopia.] I. Title.

DT373.S38 2000
963 — dc21

99-37001
CIP

Table of Contents

What if you were a giant bird soaring high above Earth? You would see huge land areas with water around them. These land areas are called **continents**. Some continents are made up of several countries. Ethiopia is in the northeastern part of the continent of Africa.

Western Hemisphere

Eastern Hemisphere

All around Ethiopia are other African countries: Somalia, Kenya, Sudan, Eritrea, and Djibouti.

Ethiopia (white) Is in The East And U.S.A. (green) is In The West

Among the bodies of water near Ethiopia are the Red Sea and the Indian Ocean.

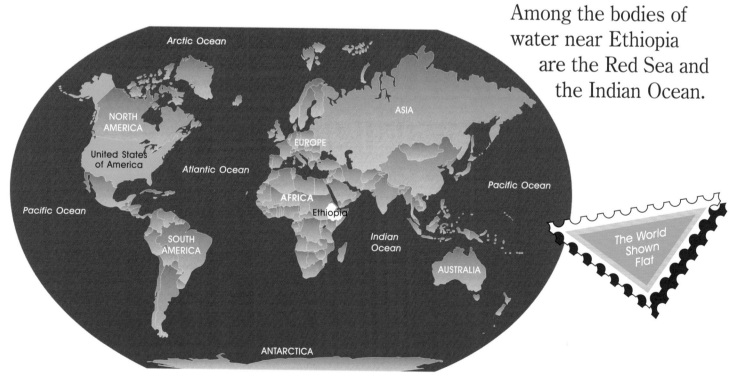

Arctic Ocean

NORTH AMERICA

United States of America

Atlantic Ocean

EUROPE

ASIA

AFRICA

Ethiopia

Pacific Ocean

Pacific Ocean

SOUTH AMERICA

Indian Ocean

AUSTRALIA

ANTARCTICA

The World Shown Flat

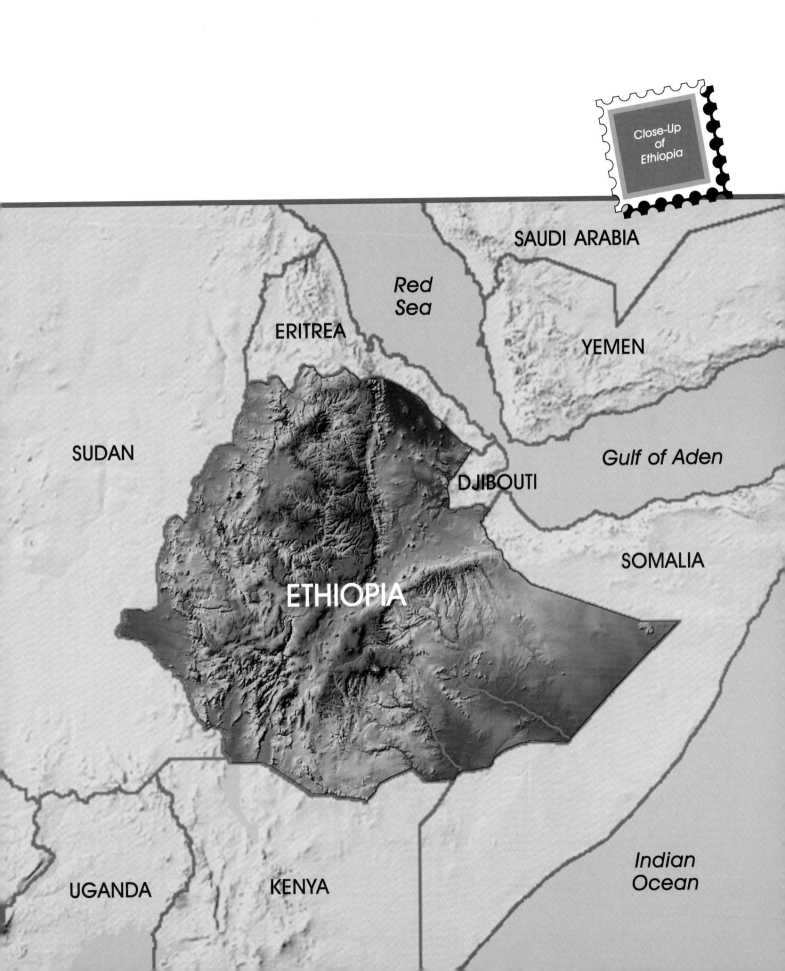

Close-Up
of
Ethiopia

SAUDI ARABIA

*Red
Sea*

ERITREA

YEMEN

SUDAN

Gulf of Aden

DJIBOUTI

SOMALIA

ETHIOPIA

UGANDA

KENYA

*Indian
Ocean*

Tissisat Falls
On The
Blue Nile
River

Lake Tana
• Lalibela
Tissisat Falls
Blue Nile River
Addis Ababa ☆
Lake Langano
EAST AFRICAN RIFT VALLEY
• Konso

The
Land

ADMIT ONE ADMIT ONE

The *East African Rift Valley* is a giant crack in the Earth. It splits Ethiopia roughly down the middle. The Rift Valley is hot and dry. So are the lowlands near Ethiopia's borders, especially in the north and east.

Northwest and southeast of the Rift Valley are mountainous highlands. They are cooler and wetter than the lowlands. Addis Ababa, Ethiopia's capital, is in the highlands northwest of the Rift Valley. So is Lake Tana, the source of the great Blue Nile River.

CORBIS/Dave Bartruff

Rolling Hills Near The Village Of Lalibela

Arid Landscape At Lake Langano

Thick grasses and forests thrive in some areas of Ethiopia where lots of rain falls. But parts of Ethiopia are semi-desert and desert, where only tough plants such as thornbushes grow. This dryness is partly because little rain falls, and partly because people chopped down too many trees and did not care for the soil when they were farming.

In many places, however, Ethiopians have planted new trees.

Among Ethiopia's animals are lions, elephants, zebras, monkeys, bush pigs, spotted hyenas, hippos, and crocodiles. Ethiopia also has birds such as eagles, golden-backed woodpeckers, white-tailed swallows, ostriches, and ibises.

CORBIS/Christiana Carvalho; Frank Lane Picture Agency

A Baobab Tree In Bloom On The Ethiopian Plateau

An Ethiopian Snipe At Lake Tana

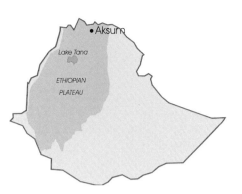

Aksum

Lake Tana

ETHIOPIAN
PLATEAU

Cacti
Growing
Along The
Ethiopian
Hills Near
Aksum

The Castle
Of
King Fasilada
At Gondar

Aksum

Gondar

Long Ago

The Bible tells of Ethiopia, one of the world's oldest countries. Some people think Solomon, King of Israel, and the Queen of Sheba had a son, *Menelik I*, who founded Ethiopia about 3,000 years ago. Others think Ethiopia is not quite that old. We do know that about 1,700 years ago, it became one of Africa's first **Christian** lands. A few hundred years later, the religion of **Islam** arrived.

For many years, emperors ruled Ethiopia. In 1896, Emperor Menelik II drove out Italians who were trying to take over. In 1930, Haile Selassie became emperor and ruled for 44 years. Haile Selassie worked hard to make life better, but during his rule the country had problems. Ethiopia was very poor. Italy invaded in 1936 and held power until 1941, when Haile Selassie regained control.

CORBIS/Paul Almasy

Haile Selassie Was Emperor Of Ethiopia from 1930 To 1974

Queen Sheba's Bath At Her Palace At Aksum

CORBIS/Roger Wood

13

Ethiopia Today

A Rebel Tank Enters Mengistu's Palace In Addis Ababa

CORBIS/Francoise de Mulder

By 1974, some people no longer wanted Emperor Haile Selassie to rule Ethiopia. They threw him out, and an army leader, Mengistu Haile Mariam, took control. Mengistu governed by **communist** ideas. This meant people could not own land— only the government owned it. People could not run businesses, either. The government ran all of the factories, banks, newspapers, and other businesses.

Prime Minister Meles Zenawi

CORBIS/Francoise de Mulder

Many people did not like communist rule, and it ended in 1991. New leaders set up a plan to make Ethiopia a **democracy**, where all people would have more freedom and power. In 1995, Meles Zenawi was elected prime minister. Since then, Ethiopia's problems have not all been solved, but people are working together on them.

☆ Addis Ababa

CORBIS/The Purcell Team

Palace Guards
In Addis
Ababa

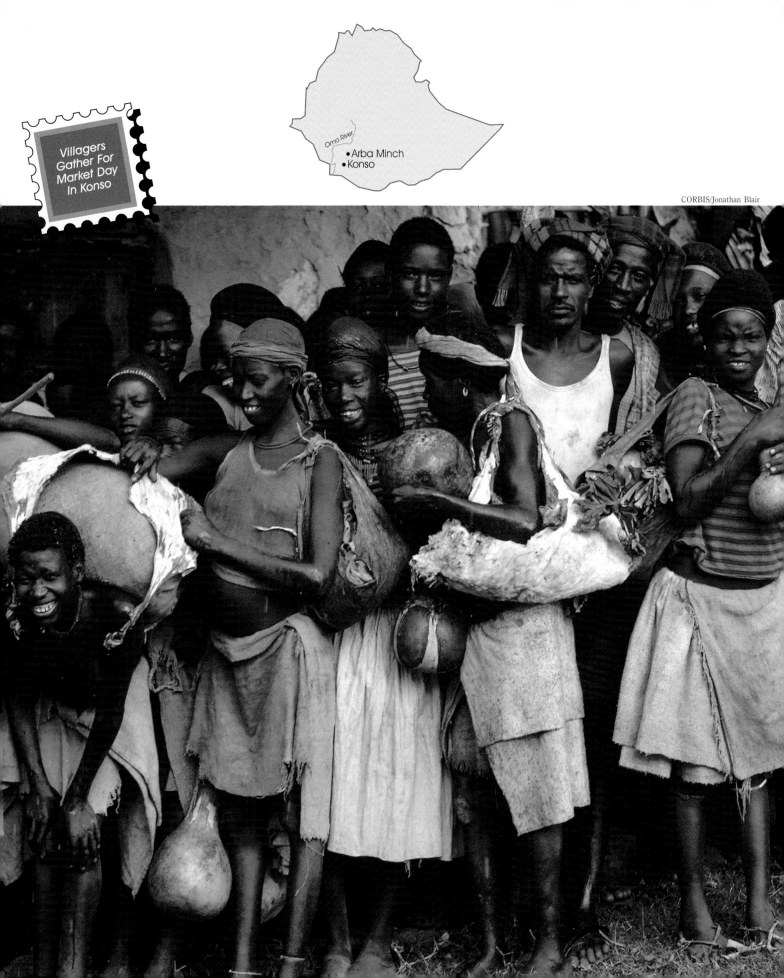

Villagers
Gather For
Market Day
In Konso

Omo River

●Arba Minch

●Konso

The People

Ethiopia is home to about 80 different groups of people. The *Amhara*, one of the largest groups, have been the most important in ruling the country. The *Tigre* and the *Oromo* are the other two large groups.

Among the smaller groups are the *Shangalla* and the *Somalis*. North of Lake Tana is a small group of Ethiopian Jews who call themselves *Beta Israel* (House of Israel).

CORBIS/Jonathan Blair

An Omo River Woman Wears A Can As A Lip Ornament

A Woman Arranges A Girl's Hair For A Ceremony In Arba Minch

CORBIS/Jim Sugar Photography

City Life
And
Country
Life

ADMIT ONE

ADMIT ONE

Sheraton Hotel In Addis Ababa

CORBIS/Dave Bartruff

Most Ethiopians live in the country in family **compounds** (groups of buildings) or villages. They build their houses of materials such as mud, mortar, and stone with a thatched or tin roof. There are very few roads in the countryside. There are very few cars, too. People walk on trails, using animals such as donkeys and camels to carry things.

A Group Of Men Transporting Goods With Donkeys

CORBIS/Carmen Redondo

Ethiopian city people have roads, buses, and some doctors and hospitals. They have modern concrete buildings such as banks, hotels, and theaters. But many city people are poor, living in crowded homes without clean water or electric lights.

CORBIS/Jim Sugar Photography

☆ Addis Ababa

● Arba Minch

Dorze
Tribespeople
In
Arba Minch

Schoolchildren
In Fasher

• Aksum

• Fasher

CORBIS/Jonathan Blair

Schools And Language

Sadly, many country Ethiopians never have the chance to go to school. Children in cities and towns have a better chance, since those areas have more schools. The government is trying to provide more schooling.

Among subjects children study in school are reading, writing, history, math, and science.

About 70 languages are spoken in Ethiopia. These include Tigrinya, Oromo, Hebrew, Somali, Arabic, and Italian. **Amharic**, the language of the Amhara, is Ethiopia's official language. Many Ethiopians learn English, too. Some people say English is Ethiopia's second official language.

A Music Shop In Aksum

CORBIS/Dave Bartruff

Work

Young Goatherds Rest On A Hillside In Arba Minch

CORBIS/Jim Sugar Photography

Most Ethiopian families are farmers or herders. The crops they grow include coffee, cotton, beans, peas, sesame seeds, and grains such as teff, wheat, and barley. The animals Ethiopians raise include sheep, goats, cattle, and chickens. Fathers usually work in the fields while mothers work at home, raising the children and making the family's food and clothes. Among the children's jobs are finding firewood, carrying water, and guarding crops against baboons.

Some Ethiopians mine gold, platinum, and marble. Some work in the forests. Others work in factories making food products, sugar, shoes, soap, and cement. Some work in restaurants, banks, and telephone offices, especially in cities.

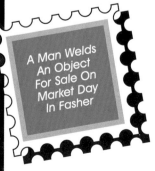
A Man Welds An Object For Sale On Market Day In Fasher

• Dirē Dawa

• Fasher

• Arba Minch

Mechanics
Working In A
At Dirē Dawa
Railway
Station

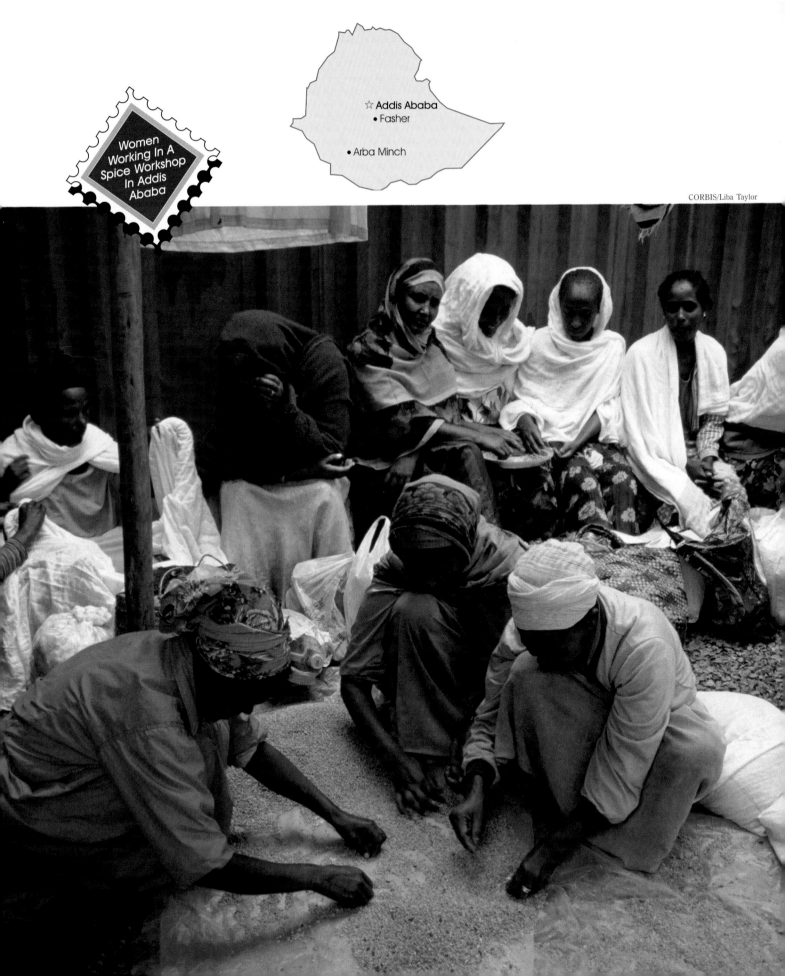

Women Working In A Spice Workshop In Addis Ababa

☆ Addis Ababa
• Fasher

• Arba Minch

CORBIS/Liba Taylor

Food

It looks like a tablecloth at an Ethiopian dinner, but it's not. It's *injera*, Ethiopia's pancake-like bread. The person serving the meal spoons other foods onto the injera. These foods include cheesy yogurt and spicy stews made with vegetables, chicken, mutton, goat, or camel. To eat it, you tear off a piece of injera, roll up some food in it, and pop it into your mouth.

Sadly, in recent years, some Ethiopians have suffered from a lack of food. Among the reasons are wars, lack of rain, and blown-away or washed-away soil. Americans and others have sent food to help starving Ethiopians.

CORBIS/Francois de Mulder

Girls Selling Fruit At A Market In Fasher

A Woman Cooking Injera In Arba Minch

CORBIS/Jim Sugar Photography

Pastimes and Holidays

Mamo Wolde Receiving A Gold Medal At The 1968 Olympic Games

CORBIS/Bettman

Ethiopians enjoy chess and *gabata,* a game something like backgammon. Soccer is the national sport. Among other sports are swimming, volleyball, horse racing, and *genna,* a kind of hockey. Ethiopian long-distance runners such as Haile GebreSelassie have won many medals in the Olympics and other competitions. In 1997, Fatima Roba became the first African woman to win the Boston Marathon.

Most of Ethiopia's holidays are religious. Among the most important is *Timkat* (the baptism of Jesus). Ethiopians also celebrate other Christian holidays such as Easter, as well as Muslim ones such as the prophet Muhammed's birth. Among non-religious holidays are New Year's Day, Labor Day, and National Day.

Ethiopians use a calendar with 12 months of 30 days and a 13th month of 5 or 6 days. Because of this, some people call Ethiopia "The Land of 13 Months of Sunshine." Sadly, in the past, many Ethiopian months have been clouded with problems such as poverty, war, disease, and lack of food. Ethiopians hope for sunnier months and years ahead—to match their sunny skies.

Deacons At A Timkat Festival In Lalibela

CORBIS/Dave Bartruff

Lalibela

Omo River

Konso

CORBIS/Jonathan Blair

Omo River
Tribespeople
Perform A
Ceremonial
Dance

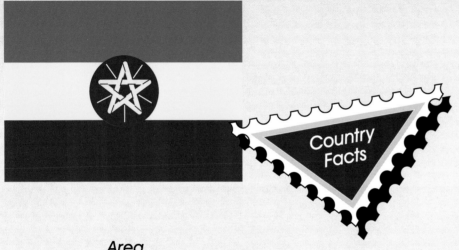

Area
About 472,000 square miles (1.2 million square kilometers)—almost twice the size of Texas.

Population
More than 60 million people.

Capital City
Addis Ababa.

Other Important Cities
Dire Dawa, Harar, and Dessie.

Money
The birr. A birr is divided into 100 cents.

National Flag
The flag has green, yellow, and red stripes. The green stripe stands for land and hope. The yellow stripe stands for church. The red stripe stands for power and faith. The star in the center has rays all the same length, showing that all of Ethiopia's people are equal. The blue behind the star stands for peace and democracy.

National Bread
Injera, a soft, pancake-like bread. It is made from *teff*, a grain native to Ethiopia and grown mainly in that nation.

Head of Government
The prime minister of Ethiopia.

Ethiopia Trivia

Did You Know?

The word "coffee" may have come from Kaffa, the Ethiopian region where many people think coffee bushes first grew. Some Ethiopians enjoy eating popcorn with their coffee.

North of Ethiopia is Eritrea, which used to be part of Ethiopia. Eritrea became a country in 1993.

Ethiopian farmers often use Zebu cattle to pull plows as well as for meat and milk. Zebu cattle have humps on their shoulders.

The name of Ethiopia's capital, Addis Ababa, means "new flower."

Ethiopians use lots of spices. Their foods are among the spiciest in Africa.

Ethiopia's official language, Amharic, is related to both Arabic and Hebrew. It has some sounds not found in English.

How Do You Say?

	AMHARIC	HOW TO SAY IT
Hello	t'ena yïst 'ïlliñ	(tuh-yay-naw ih-stuh-eel-een-yuh)
Good-bye	dähna huñi	(duh-naw hoon-yuh-ee)
Please	asdässätä	(aws-duh-suh-tuh)
Thank You	ïgzer yïmmäsgän	(eegz-yayr yih-muhs-guhn)
One	and	(awnd)
Two	hulätt	(hool-uht)
Three	sost	(swost)
Ethiopia	Ityopia	(eet-ywo-puh-yaw)

Amharic (am–HAYR–ik)
Amharic is the official language of Ethiopia. It is related to the Arabic and Hebrew languages.

Christian (KRISS–chen)
A Christian is a person who believes in the teachings of Jesus Christ. Ethiopia was one of the first Christian lands in Africa.

communist (KOM–yoo–nist)
When a government is communist, it owns all of the land and businesses in a country. Ethiopia has had communist rulers in the past.

compounds (KOM–pownds)
Compounds are small groups of houses or buildings. Some country people in Ethiopia live in compounds.

continents (KON–tih–nents)
Earth's land areas are divided up into huge sections called continents. Ethiopia is part of the continent of Africa.

democracy (deh–MAH–kra–see)
A democracy is a form of government where the people of a country vote for their leaders and laws. Ethiopia is a democracy.

Islam (is–LAHM)
Islam is a set of beliefs about God (called Allah) and his prophet Muhammad. Some Ethiopians belong to the Islamic faith.

Index

Web Sites

Learn more about Ethiopia:
http://www.nicom.com/~ethiopia/ove.htm

Visit the Embassy of Ethiopia in Washington, D.C.:
http://www.ethiopianembassy.org

Listen to the Ethiopian national anthem:
http://www.travelwise.org/Anthems/ethiopia.htm

Learn how to make injera:
http://www.cs.indiana.edu/hyplan/dmulholl/ethiopia/Injera_english.html